Ignited Ink 717 Presents

ignite Her

Ignited Ink 717 Presents

Ignite Her

Poetry Collection

Featuring poetry by EbonyRose,
Renee Blackwell, Sarahtonin, Skyy Danielle,
& Tequila Smith

Ignited Ink 717 LLC

Ignited Ink 717 LLC
Houston, TX

Cover Design: Ebony Rose of Ignited Ink 717 LLC

Categories: Poetry/Professional Development

Contributing Poets:
Ebony R. Smith, LaTrice Jenkins, Sarah Wagner, Skyy Danielle, Tequila Smith

EbonyRose, Renee Blackwell, Sarahtonin, Skyy Danielle, and Tequila Smith are available for performances, keynotes, panels, book talks, and workshops.

Discounts for bulk purchases of 25 books or more are available.
Visit IgnitedInk717.com to learn more and place an order.

For reprint permission, write to IgnitedInk717@gmail.com

ISBN (PRINT): 979-8-9909403-6-9

Printed in the United States of America

Dedication

To every woman before us who was brave enough to
pick up a pen, thank you for passing the torch.

We vow to keep our Ink Ignited.

Preface

Poetry is fire—unruly, transformative, and impossible to ignore. *Ignite-Her* is not just a collection of poems; it is a testament to the power of women wielding words like flames. Born from the 30for30 challenge held annually to celebrate National Poetry Month, Ignited Ink 717 decided to immortalize this ink in eternity. This anthology is five women poets, thirty days, and an unrelenting commitment to igniting their creativity.

EbonyRose, Renee Blackwell, Sarahtonin, Skyy Danielle, and Tequila Smith did more than write; they created a fiery moment. Each poet provided prompts, setting the stage for a collective wildfire of expression. Every day, one poet answered the call, breathing life into language, turning blank pages into embers that spark reflection, resilience, and revolution.

This is poetry as resistance. Poetry as healing. Poetry as the match struck against silence. Let these verses burn away doubt.

Let them remind you that every woman carries a flame within her—waiting, ready, undeniable.

And now, you are invited to join the blaze. Throughout this book, you'll find blank pages—spaces for you to spill your own ink, to let the prompts move through you, to set fire to the page with your truth. If a prompt ignites your ink, share your poem with Ignited Ink 717 by tagging @ignitedink717.

This is more than a book. It's a movement. A wildfire of voices rising together. Stay IGNITED.

TABLE OF
Contents

TABLE OF

Contents

Day 01

Prompt

Write a humorous poem where you are facing judgment day. The only way to prevent damnation is to confess all of your sins or to hypnotize the executioner.

Include: funny bone, laugh out loud, and comedy club

EbonyRose

Confess-Her

I can tell God's patience has never been thinner,

Call me opposite over hypotenuse, cuz I've been a

sinner!

The Executioner is ready; all my mistakes he has

seen,

So to prevent damnation, I have to come clean.

Though these confessions will leave me wearing the

shame cone,

I sure hope these humorous sins tickle God's funny

bone!

Forgive me, Father, for I have sinned;

sorry, Sky Daddy, I've been naughty,

I spent my young life being exceptionally thotty.

I used innocent people when I didn't know what I

wanted,

Now all the souls I ghosted are forever haunted.

When I was mad at my mother, though I wasn't a crook,

I wrote "infection" next to every "yeast" in her favorite cookbook!

I made so many promises I never fulfilled,

So I now understand why my presence wasn't much of a thrill.

I pushed away those who truly cared about me,

Yet held onto toxic ones that never made me feel free.

Every time I eat soup, I'll admit, I do slurp,

And during church sermon, I let out a loud burp!

I've blamed things on others that I had done,

I fell asleep in the bar bathroom after too much "fun",

I didn't pay attention in Psychology class;

My professor was hot, and I stared at her ass!

Executioner, I can tell you're giving me quite the snub,

You're scorning like a heckler at the Comedy Club!

I'll admit, the old me had the personality of a fart,

But at least I can turn my mistakes into art!

I debated saving myself by putting you under a spell,

But I figured you'd let me go if I give you an LOL.

I'm the first to admit I've made many mistakes,

I hope you'll realize my afterlife is at stake.

While you ponder my fate, I'll leave you alone,

But remember, He who is without sin may cast the first stone.

Day 02

Prompt

Write an acrostic for the name of the most

influential person in your life (past or present)

Sarahterin

'DOROTHY'

December dances with a yearning for a love that now lacks resonance

Only the gift of warm embrace and ringlets would suffice

Righteous and worthy, your essence divine

October birthed a being abnormally otherworldly, so I celebrate with you spiritually .

Tables filled with offerings, I am ready to receive your guidance

Humble, I present myself

You, dear mom, are my greatest muse and if I could grow into half the woman that you were then I'd be stronger than I ever thought that I could be.

Day 83

Prompt

Write a poem about a particular fragrance or odor
from your past that triggers a memory. Where in
your mind does it take you? Would you like to
return to that place? Would you like to speak to
that person one more time?

Tequila Smith

Ignite

Is it getting hot in here or have you just met your

match!? Let today's prompt IGNITE your INK.

We want to feature your poem. Tag @IgnitedInk717

Day 04

Prompt

Write a poem about the process of becoming a

woman.

Ignite-Her

Grøw-Her

She is a seed

Embracing her stages of dormancy

Germinating into a seedling

Pushing pass the dirt

In search of water

Gasping for air

Pleading for air

Growing and growing

She can be expansive

She can fill an entire field

While filtering toxins and pollutants

Being a source of food

Or simply basking in the beauty of existing

Even if you trim parts of her

She'll grow back more lush than before

She never stops growing

Even when the seasons change

She may fade and fall away

But she will still be there

Under the blankets of fresh snow

Patiently waiting for her signal to grow

Day 85

Prompt

Write a poem looking at your reflection.

What do you see?

Skyy Danielle

Her Reflection

I am staring at her,

And she is gazing back at me.

Does she know I once struggled to love her?

That I wished that she looked like someone else?

Could she ever forgive me for missing her obvious

beauty?

It took others to point it out.

Her golden skin, slanted eyes, and full lips.

I had to see her beauty in others who were a

reflection of her.

I love her now more than ever.

I wish it hadn't taken me so long.

Could she ever forgive me for missing her obvious

beauty?

Her golden skin slanted eyes and full lips.

I am staring at her, and she is gazing back at me.

She is golden, soft, slant eyes, and full lips.

She has a smile that will put you in a trance

And an oceanic sway in her hips.

She is fierce! Sophisticated,

Confident,

Talented,

Passionate,

And unapologetic.

She is golden,

Soft,

Slanted eyes and full lips.

She is unapologetically ME.

Day 86

Prompt

Write a poem about the part of yourself that
terrifies you. You must reflect and be honest with
yourself. How did or will you turn that dark part
of yourself into someone you want to love and
share a space with?

Renee Blackwell

Mɒnst-Her

You are the thing nightmares are made of

the type of darkness that light doesn't have the

courage to venture to

the type of darkness that keeps the boogeyman up

at night,

causing him to seek sanctuary under our beds.

You are a horrid Horcrux, murderous, magic,

all deathly and hollow.

I thought you would perish in the pit.

I abandoned you ages ago.

I still remember how you would gorge on violence,

how the gore was your glory.

You are a beast, untamed.

The thought of you makes my soul tremble.

As a safety precaution,

I bury you beneath the other cheek,

beneath smiles and good intentions.

I never tried to love you.

I guess I could at least try.

I just realized.

You'll only make the earth bleed.

To protect me.

Day 07

Prompt

Write a poem that explains a time in your life when

you decided to change

Ignite-Her

Metaphor-phosis

The caterpillar

turns into a butterfly

in the chrysalis

What they don't tell you:

They turn to goo

before they become butterflies

And this is to say:

The transformation only happens

post-breakdown

The muscle breaks down

after the workout before

solidifying

You are not broken;

God is pouring the plaster

of your newest form

I found spoken word

at my lowest, then became

a published author

The stage returned my

voice to my body and took

the knife out my hands

Lonely Friday nights

made me invest in myself

and what my heart needs

My few connections

fulfill my heart in ways my

"party friends" would not

My love found me in

pieces and quickly became

my sweet peace of mind

I replaced bottles

with such beautiful bonds

that rehydrate my soul

Though lost in the mail,

my bright smile was finally

returned to sender

Every time I start

to slip into old habits,

I remind myself

All of my actions

Have equal and opposite

reactions, which means

Future me will pay

the price for the bad choices

I currently make

Long-term success takes

precedence over instant

gratification

I closed the door on

a life that did not serve me;

blessings now pour in

Because I transformed,

I am now living the life

that I once prayed for

Day 88

Prompt

Write A haiku about PMS

Sarahtonin

ignite

Is it getting hot in here or have you just met your

match!? Let today's prompt IGNITE your INK.

We want to feature your poem. Tag @IgnitedInk717

Day 89

Prompt

Write a poem about aging. Do you fear the process
of aging? What does life look life for you as an
elder?

Renee Blackwell

Twilight

I sat at the table for the longest time,

enjoying the melody.

Then Twilight waltzed over

and he decided to dance with me.

I knew he'd eventually come my way

as he dances with everyone.

If you happen to stick around,

you better believe he's coming.

From him, you can not run.

I stood up and took my place on the dance floor.

I danced so gracefully.

Though I've seen Twilight dance quite aggressively

with some, he is very kind to me.

So, I'm a little leery about how long this dance
might be,

If I can keep it up,

Or will Twilight take over me?

Please, God, don't let me ache and wither from
being in too much pain.

Cause I heard that Twilight can do that to folks for
whom he's called out their name.

Some people had been practicing for their dance
with Twilight,

As they knew he would surely come.

I've also practiced from time to time.

I hope it pays off

Cause I don't feel like I'm done.

So I looked Twilight in his eyes and said,

 "I'm gonna do what I can to slow you down."

I hope you like this melody, my dude,

Cause I plan to stick around.

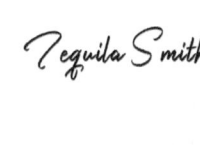

Day 18

Prompt

Write a poem about a moment when you felt overwhelmingly joyful. Try to convey this emotion by depicting the setting, the time, and what prompted this strong feeling of happiness and joy.

Tequila Smith

Frozen Sunshine

Most days go by in a blur

no noticeable notions or traces of significance

In my 13,000-plus days here on earth

I remember the happiest one

The day the sky cracked open and released a piece

of Heaven

The day I cracked open and received love for the

first time

Holding the coldest joy near my chest

feeling my heart fill up with angel's voices

the ice melting from within

the day I held Winter and became an Auntie.

34

Day 11

Prompt

Write a poem standing up to a bully.

Plot twist: the bully is YOU!

She Said

She said

You think you're the shit huh?!

More like the shit on the bottom of my shoe

You let me walk all over you

You're the animal in my zoo

You allow me to keep you caged from your natural

habitat so now I can control people's perception of

you

She said

Their perception of you is more important than

your perception of you because there's no

exception for the things that you do

So just try to blend in

Because you're way overdue on this process of

healing

So chin up

Shoulders back

Drop those feelings

There's no time to cry

Put your mental health aside

Fuck your pride

There is no try

Just continue to mope around being dry

She said

What's this talk about you trying to mold yourself

back together?

Bitch it's giving Humpty Dumpty!

Can you not see that you are forever broken?

You've got to be joking!

She said

I own you!

You have been mastered by the whips and chains of

the words I exclaim

You're nothing more than a fake

claim to fame and to name

the only notable achievement you've gained

is pretending to be ok knowing you're drained

I Said

Mirror mirror on the wall

Why is she trying to play us like we don't stand tall

Like we don't have it all

Like I don't love me and all my flaws

Girl don't you know that I am you

That there's nothing new you can say or do

If I don't want to receive it

I don't have to

Just in case you don't understand

You march to the beat of my band

You're not directing shit

Skyy Danielle

Day 12

Prompt

Write a poem describing the taste of sunshine.

Skyy Danielle

Citrus

Whispers of sun rays softly brush my face

With my head titled back and lips slightly parted

I accept this intimacy

I crave it, really.

Because Sunshine tastes like love

Even when the clouds are soft and dark

I still fill the black hole and emptiness that love

brings to me.

Who am I without it, after all?

Sunshine tastes like her

A shadow looming over my heart

Sweet and savory, her kisses cut like knives

I love sharp objects

I've become accustomed to burning myself

And healing myself just to prove that no one else

can take care of me like I can

Because sunshine tastes like mangoes

I rip through the flesh with my teeth

Letting the juices flow down my chin

Sunshine tastes like her

Or perhaps it tastes like Louisiana

The sweaty air still hangs on my tongue.

I'll never get that freedom I felt as my body rolled

down the hill.

Laughter, bugs, and traffic became my soundtrack.

Memories are memories, whether painful or

endearing.

I've tasted sunshine, rain and snow.

I've tasted blood, tears and sweat.

I've tasted life and kissed death.

Above all, sunshine is internal and eternal.

Sunshine is consistency.

A new day to get life right.

It absolutely, undeniably tastes like that moment
when you start to grieve.

Sunshine tastes like my mother.

Day 13

Prompt

Write A free-verse from the perspective of loaded

cheese fries

Sarahtonin

Le Carnaval

It's an interesting position to be in

to indeed be the hottest thing at the fair

dripping queso to the flo'

building mountains and Castles,

depending on the artistic ability at your disposal.

Hey, corn dog, ain't nobody coming to see you.

Otis!

What a time to be alive under the flashing lights,

the cheer and the flare exploding at every corner.

For a moment, I am transported into their world,

I knew this day would come

when someone would crave me down to the last

crumb.

Someone whose eyes can behold my gooey goodness
and marvel at my garnish.
This is the moment I dreamed of since I became a
small fry, and all that dreaming could not have
prepared me for what would come next.

What happens when your sauce grows cold,
when your crunch is now a soggy memory,
when they can no longer hold you in one hand
and fun in the other,
when you are not allowed on the ride,
when you are tossed in the bin to be forgotten

Day 14

Prompt

Write a poem that personifies peace.

POV: Peace Only Vibes

The clouds glide above

Reality is breezy

Takes me to the sun

Flows with the season

She resembles harmony

Sun rays bring her hope

Sunrise brings new hope

Embrace beauty and the beast

Then you'll obtain peace

Day 15

Prompt

Write a poem about GOD. Your intimacy with
Him. Your relationship with GOD. What do you
love about GOD? What questions do you still have
about Him? For Him? What do you fear about
GOD? What about GOD brings you peace?

Tequila Smith

Girl Meets God

Whenever I think of God, I think of Mr. Feeny from "Boy Meets World".

His encyclopedia brain and all-powerful knowledge, his patience with even the toughest of students that seem to be sent by Satan himself, and above all, his ability to turn the simplest of conversations into life lessons viewers from the 90's carry with them for eternity.

Growing up, the stash of tape recordings on top of the VCR was my bible.

When I needed guidance, rather than turning to Samuel 2:16, I turn to Season 2 Episode 16.

You see, my parents tried to typewrite

Galations 1:10 onto my blank brain, but when Mr.

Feeny tells young Cory the same lesson,

"If you let people's perception of you dictate your

behavior, you will never grow as a person,"

somehow it sets in with so much strength.

Even as an adult, sometimes I feel like 12 year old

Cory trying to navigate through the hallways of

adulthood, thinking the secret code to

understanding the world around me is inside this

locker that I was somehow assigned without being

given the combination, and just like the locker's

knob, most of the time, I don't know where to turn.

But Mr. Feeny's Social Studies Session was my Sunday Service, the first desk in the middle row where Topanga sat was my front-row seat closest to the pastor,and Mr. Feeny's never-ending one-liner life lessons became my favorite bible verses.

When I think of walking and talking with our Creator, I think of crossing over into Mr. Feeny's yard for a late night talk, just like when Cory failed his exam after staying up late with his dad to watch the game.

I grew up believing I would be eternally punished for failing the trials life gave me in my younger years, but now I think of God as a teacher, a guide in the right direction, one to sit and talk with and

know that even if I failed once before, I am still valued, loved, and worthy of a second chance, and my mistakes are not damnation, but rather redirection.

I think of God as a neighbor, someone you can call on to borrow some words of wisdom or even just a cup of sugar, someone to watch over you and your life from behind the fence and to guard you with a hedge of protection when you're away.

I never understood the notion that we needed to present ourselves a certain way to be in the presence of our Creator when He's right in our own backyard, ready for us to come home and hear about our day.

It makes sense we are called to Love Thy Neighbor
As Thyself as we are created in His image.

Like Mr. Feeny, I like to think God is proud of us
just for being who we are.

Just like Mr. Feeny selecting Cory for the 6th grade
Geography bowl, hoping to take home yet another
first place but upon losing, choosing to place Cory's
A+ in the spot where the award would've gone,

I like to think God whispers in our ear, "I love you,
not because of your accomplishments, not because
of the titles you've earned, but because you exist.
You are beautifully and wonderfully made, and
that's more than enough for me."

I always wondered why my trials made me feel so alone, like the classroom of empty desks on the season finale as we hear Mr. Feeny dismiss his class one last time, wondering why I'd seemingly been equipped with every tool I'd need to succeed yet I felt like God was failing me despite the work I'd done.

Why wouldn't he answer my questions?
Where was my guide?

But though Mr. Feeny taught his students every lesson they'd need, the teacher is always
silent during the test.

I like to think in some alternate universe, Mr. Feeny still watches over his former students who have now

taken on the tests of the world, still keeps his gate open a crack in case they need a guide in the right direction, who need a listening ear when work, family, or other tribulations wear on them heavier than their elementary school Geography textbooks from their earlier years, whose inner child would still give anything to hear him say he's proud of them one more time.

I bet He'd still give them A pluses with gold star stickers upon their successes; His way of saying, "Faithful servant, well done."

Day 16

Prompt

Write a poem that is a body language cheat sheet.

Skyy Danielle

Body 101

Whooodaaawhooo, thank you for joining me!

Welcome to, Body Language 101, for dummies

by the end of this course, you'll be able to hear

words unspoken and be fluent in 'her-body-nese'.

Her body is always speaking in whispers, in woes.

In warnings. In wisdom.

We just have to listen to transcribe the lesson

If you lock eyes with a woman, and her smile

escapes her face and she looks away

She is searching for an escape route out of the

interaction

It is not an invitation to invade her space

The gravity of you in her orbit,

will cause her to crash land

If you sit next to a woman and she pulls her arms in

and makes her knees meet for prayer

It is not a new testament to your god-like stature

more of a sermon about the sins of man.

A cry for salvation.

A prayer that something or someone will become a

red sea stopping your advances.

This is the part of the lesson most fail

Her body gives room for interpretation,

but her mouth speaks gospel

If she says she's not interested,

SHE'S NOT INTERESTED

If she says stop,

STOP!

If she says no,

THAT MEANS NO!

If she says she is not willing to sacrifice her body,

find someone else to crucify...

Class dismissed.

Day 17

Prompt

Write a poem placing the last person that hurt you

on trial.

The verdict must be: FORGIVEN

EbonyRose

61

The Absolution of Renee'

If my abuser must take the stand

I will be beside her

Fueled with hate and shame

And blame

I am anchored to her in a

A sea of blood that I've shed throughout the years

Red waves throwing every secret to shore

The pressure of the belt marks suffocating me

Waking on the floor realizing that she wants me

dead

I should have felt invincible, strong because I lived

But instead tears were shed for her

A failure at best

She was never meant to be anything

but what she let the world create her to be.

If my abuser must take the stand

I have to.

Because the truth is

We are one.

We are guilty

We have done hateful things and we must take

accountability.

Because I don't deserve the abuse but she doesn't

deserve the things that made her that way.

The struggle to want to thrive but die

within a moment

feels like being anchored in a sea of transgressions.

They float about

Haunting

And taunting me.

the waves crash against me

I must make a decision

Drown or forgive the person on trial

So, in this moment.

I chose to forgive myself.

Renee Blackwell

Day 18

Prompt

Imagine you're conversing with Poetry.

What would you say? How would you feel?

Where does the conversation take place?

Speak your truth in this poem, Poet!

Renee Blackwell

Ignite

Is it getting hot in here or have you just met your match!? Let today's prompt IGNITE your INK.

We want to feature your poem. Tag @IgnitedInk717

Day 19

Prompt

Write a poem about your skin. The appearance,

feel, smell, and taste. Include the imperfections and

what you love about your skin.

Tequila Smith

Tattoo

My father gazes upon the newest inked image injected into my skin, the delicate doodle that danced across my dermis and declares, "You really need to stop with the tattoos; it's not a good look."

He seems to not understand that the body is a temple, and our good God gives us the free will to decorate our temple with the creations we collect in the space between our temples.

What is a museum without its mounted masterpieces?

What is a display without its designs dancing from door to door?

Just like the symbols scrawled across my skin, though I am a work in progress, I am still a work of art.

My first tattoo was a matchy with my best friend Ashley; a penguin with a small heart on my shoulder.

On the days where life's loneliness lingers like artic air, I will maintain this campfire of a heart.

Even when I feel more stuck than a flightless bird, when I feel more isolated than an igloo, I glue myself to the fact that no matter how I may feel in the moment, I am so, so loved.

In 2022, I got the Encanto candle etched into my left arm the way the movie is etched into my heart.

I know how it feels to only be valued as a light source for others, to fear friends forming into foes upon failure to flourish.

But just like a candle's flame, any spark that is extinguished can always be re-lit.

Even when I find myself trapped in a house of darkness, there is always a light at the end of the candle wic, and the miracle is not some magic that I've got, the miracle is me.

"Still I Rise, December 11th 2019" has made a home on my right shoulder.

For years, I thought I'd never rise from the field of hellfire I'd fallen into.

Until recent years, it seemed the only things that had risen in me were wrath, resentment, and the razor scars on my skin, but just when the fire in my spirit appears to have burned out, out of the ashes I will rise, sending a smoke signal to everyone that tried to put me out, because in the words of Earl the Poet, you can't put this flame out, baby!

So, no, dad, I will not stop with the tattoos. It's not a "good look", it's a perfect look because it's my look

My skin is a museum molded from marvelous memories marked by ink masters, a canvas constantly collecting colorful creations, a tell-all of temporary turmoil turned testimony.

I shall share the script of my story on my skin, and my soul will never cease to shine.

Sarahtonin

Day 20

Prompt

Write a eulogy for a trait you once had that no

longer serves you.

Sarahtonin

So Long Self-Doubt

We gather here today to say farewell and good riddance to a relentless adversary that has plagued my mind for far too long: Self-doubt.

I must admit that letting go of self-doubt is not going to be easy.
Self-doubt was a comfort to me.

I would run to it anytime I was faced with a challenge.
It was dependable and constant.
It afforded me excuses.
With self-doubt, I didn't even have to try.
And I was okay with that.

But then I got tired of watching others get the breaks I should have gotten.

They got the appreciation and recognition that I knew I deserved.

I started to realize that self-doubt was holding me back.

When I said, "I could",
 self-doubt said, "I couldn't."
When I said, "I would,"
self-doubt said, "I wouldn't."
When I felt that I was enough,
self-doubt made me feel as if I was less than.

Self-doubt was never my friend.

So I am walking away with my head held high.
I feel a weight has been lifted off me already.
So long Self-doubt

With a light heart, I commemorate its passing

and celebrate the freedom it leaves in its wake.

Self-doubt, though a formidable foe, could not

withstand my courage,

Confidence,

Resilience,

And belief in myself that ultimately triumphed.

May its departure serve as a reminder to everyone

of our own strength and ascendancy,

As I forge ahead with confidence and dominance in

all my endeavors.

Rest in peace, self-doubt.

Your presence will not be missed.

Day 21

Prompt

Write a poem that explores life from the perspective

of a seed.

Nature VX Nurture

I've nurtured nature

Whispered ,"I love you"to the tiny seeds

as I tucked them into the soil

We shared water, space and time.

Alas, a small green stem appeared and shortly died.

Perhaps, it was my fault

Perhaps, it was not the right season

Yet, I persisted.

I whispered,"I love you"again

to a new tiny seed that was tucked in with soil.

I was determined for growth

The place where seeds go to die was not an option.

Many seeds have died

Just as I have

Many seeds have lived

Just as I have

I've nurtured my nature

A seed that grows in darkness will soon see light

and thrive.

Is there hope for the seedling that was never meant

to survive?

Day 22

Prompt

Write a poem that is an ad for therapy.

Include: a 1-800 number and a list of 'side effects'

Swipe Right

Imagine exploring the world of dating

You finally decide to give that app a try

You get caught in the rhythm of swiping left

Then you see that perfect one

The one whose aura reflects that of your mated soul

Someone who holds a mirrror of guided reflection

So you swipe right for a chance

to feel seen, heard, and understood

Finally!

The real one

The one that listens

The one that stays

The one you have those late-night conversations

that turn into early morning revelations with

Vibrations syncing with your heartbeat like your favorite 90's R&B song
that fills you with the feel of a Real Love
Alignment at its finest

Let's set the scene
You arrive to a picnic in the park
It's cozy, breeze just right, nature's love all around
serving its purpose

You sit down and there's no pressure to be anyone
but yourself
It's like a first date where there's no need to impress
Just express

You talk, they listen

You open up, they hold space

It's vulnerability without fear
Intimacy without judgement

It's that relationship that allows the weight you
carried to grow wings

Where you unpack your past
Sort through the mess and see the beauty in your
scars

Learning to love yourself
Flaws and all
This is what you call life with therapy

Please be aware that the side effects of entering

into this partnership may include but are not

limited to:

Feeling exposed and raw some days

Taking accountability for self

Facing moments of discomfort

Becoming acquainted with your inner critic

Releasing forgiveness

Setting boundaries

Vibrating on a higher frequency

Harmonizing with confidence

Experiencing nights of deep, restful sleep,

Allowing a newfound strength to take root

A new perception that allows you to see the world's

colors more vividly

Just to name a few

Imagine the healing, the empowerment.

It's like finding someone

who loves you at your worst

Celebrates you at your best

And sticks around for all the in-betweens

Therapy is your partner in self-discovery

Your guide in the journey to wholeness

And when you look in the mirror

You'll see someone who's been through the fire and

emerged stronger

Someone who's found peace in their reflection

And now you're more than just surviving; you're

thriving

CALL 1-800-HEAL-NOW

Because you deserve to be seen, heard, and to give

your worries their wings.

Let's swipe right

on healing together!

Day 23

Prompt

Write about your first experience with death. It
could be a person, pet, or character. How'd it affect
you? Do you think it solidified your view of the
concept of dying and how you grieve?

Renee Blackwell

Masked Depression

In the stillness of a somber night,

A soul moved on, out of sight,

Leaving behind a painful void

that was heavy in its weight,

As she left everyone in a mournful state.

It was my mother's closest friend,

Whose pain transcended to life's end,

Through depression and heartache that ran so deep,

She sought a solace she could keep.

Her struggles masked by her smiling face

Each day, an internal battle she had to face

Yet, no refuge could she find,

In the recesses of her mind

Her journey ended, and she was gone

A final chapter, her journey, so long

Yet, in her leaving, there's release,

Though bittersweet, she is at peace.

For me, I questioned how and why

Wasn't there anyone whom she could rely,

I questioned the nature of our final breath,

And how we navigate the path of death.

It taught me to embrace life,

The good and the bad

To honor loss and the life once had

To grieve in ways both light and deep,

To find in sorrow, moments to keep.

Though sadness cloaked my mother's heart,

I sensed relief, a brand new start,

For her friend had found her forever peace

Amidst the realms of eternity.

Day 24

Prompt

Write a poem from the perspective of a cloud.

describe the sky.

Skyy Danielle

Don't Rain on My Parade

Good evening everyone!

I hope everyone's having a great fluffing night!

I'd like to introduce myself.

My name is Q. Mulus, and being here has got me on

Cloud 10!

It's like Cloud 9, but even higher!

I don't like to rain on anyone's parade, but

sometimes I suffer from (b)rain fog,

so if I get a little hazy,

please whether the weather with me until I get a

brain storm and my train of thought returns.

Sometimes when I need some air, I'll go into my safe

space up in the sky and listen to music to calm the

thunderstorm in me. I call it my Airpod.

Despite my struggles, there are so many beautiful parts of my life that fill me with more sparks than a lightning storm!

My cousin Q. Mulonimbus and I like to look at people and determine their shape like people do with us clouds.

One time someone thought I was shaped like a horse with 2 legs, but someone else said I was shaped like a TV tray.

One time, my cousin said someone was shaped like a person with daddy issues, but I thought it was shaped like a chronic people pleaser.

Another time, I thought someone was shaped like a workaholic, but my cousin said, "Nah, bro, that's a Capricorn".

It's interesting how no one's perspective is neither right nor wrong, just different depending on your own lived experiences.

I love when the sky is cotton candy colored.
Even when I feel sky blue, I'm always tickled pink when the sky paints itself into a masterpiece just for me.

I find it so funny how we're always looking up to someone for inspiration without realizing we also have people looking up to us.

There's always a new level to reach, from the troposphere to the exosphere and everything in between.

There have been many times I've tried to reach for the sky, but I mist the mark, and unfortunately, it left me with an intense anxiety around elevating higher than the ground, also known as stratos-fear.

But I just push through this layer of anxiety like a rocketship pushing through the layers of the atmosphere, and I always reach my destination.

I hope you enjoyed my story, and that none of this went over your head like me and my cousin while we're guessing people shapes!

I want to leave you with words of encouragement.

There may be times when life has a gray outlook and you may feel like you're drifting away from your true self, but I promise, there's always a silver lining.

Don't be afraid to take up space. Whether you're a solid, liquid, or gas, or all 3 like me, you matter.

And if anyone ever tries to make you feel like you don't, you just tell them, "Hail no, get away from me! No one can wind-break me! Because with me, the sky's the limit, and I'll always rain supreme!"

Sarahtonin

Day 25

Prompt

Write a poem about outgrowing someone. It can be
a lover, a friend, or perhaps it's not someone, but
something. Include the conflict between your heart
and your mind to decide to leave.

Tequila Smith

Out of a Limb

I am an old oak tree.

My bark groans and my branches ache.
The fruits I carved in my seedling heart have rotten
away.

Leaves I thought would be with me forever are gone
in the wind.

I heard someone mention the pruning process
how it encourages healthy fruit to grow by
removing dead branches.

But I don't remember mourning for you.
no ashes for your beauty.

When did you die?

How did I not notice?

Was it when I branched out into a new forest and met trees that talked amongst the stars?

Or when I began to whisper poetry to the wind?

Or when I began to work on my core and sunk my roots deeper into the ancestor soil?

Haven't we been connected this whole time?

You've been a part of me as long as I could remember.

I held on to you as long as I could

allowed the splinters to dig deeper into my flesh

phantom of the things we wood be

etched into our hands.

My limbs, would never be the same.

Ebony Rose

Day 26

Prompt

Write A humorous limerick

Sarahterin

ignite

Is it getting hot in here or have you just met your match!? Let today's prompt IGNITE your INK.

We want to feature your poem. Tag @IgnitedInk717

Day 27

Prompt

What does it feel like to fly?

Boundless Sky

I am free

soaring high above the ground

Weightless

No gravity to hold me down

I am lifted by the wind

Above negativity, pettiness, jealousy, and hate

I am winning

My blessings await.

In this boundless sky, I find my peace,

Where worries fade, and troubles are ceased.

With each breath of untainted air,

a newfound grace,

Only God's favored can share,

in this sacred space.

No chains can bind, no limits define,

As I soar above these beautiful clouds

Watch my success and the attraction of crowds.

In the beauty of flight, my determination is stirred.

Nothing but God's words can be heard.

With wings unfurled, I embrace this flight

Guided by His words, my future, shining so bright.

As I fly through the air

Success innate

I will not look back because my blessings await.

Day 28

Prompt

Write a poem using the phrase, 'Wrong way'.

Skyy Danielle

Redirect

The doubt of my love leads her astray

On a quest to find a heart where her hand may lay.

I swore, I killed, I pillaged and fought

Yet, I stand screaming but no words would come

out

My darling, I've committed crimes,

How is it that you find my dedication asinine?

She responds with words in kind.

Your lack of words are what led me a stray.

You love me, this I know

But you loved me the wrong way

You're a poet,

Your words destroy heartbreaks.

How is it that you've filled the paper with such
passion and courage that you've have nothing left
for me?

Renee Blackwell

Day 29

Prompt

Write a poem using these words: tacenda, soil,

water, perish, and caution.

Renee Blackwell

Soil

The soil of one's truth

Fed water to the masses

with deep reverence

Caution them to speak

For their voice holds the lesson

As the false perish

Respect will surface

Judgement becomes tacenda

On freedoms command

Day 38

Prompt

Write a poem describing a life where every day is a
celebration.

ignite

Is it getting hot in here or have you just met your
match!? Let today's prompt IGNITE your INK.

We want to feature your poem. Tag @IgnitedInk717

Stay Ignited!

About the Authors

EbonyRose

EbonyRose is a creative, poet, visionary, entrepreneur, author and mental health advocate. A nationally ranked spoken word artist, slam poetry champion, and literary architect, she wields language like fire, igniting truth in every syllable. As the founder and visionary behind Ignited Ink 717, she has carved a space where the historically silenced are not only heard but amplified, where ink becomes resistance and storytelling becomes revolution. @EbonyRoseOut

Ignited Ink 717

Ignited Ink 717 is an independent publishing house devoted to amplifying the voices of the historically silenced. With a fierce commitment to storytelling that sparks change, we provide a platform for authors whose words challenge, inspire, and ignite the world. Through intentional publishing, we celebrate diverse narratives, ensuring that every story finds its light and every voice is heard.

@IgnitedInk717

About the Authors

Renee Blackwell

Renee' Blackwell is a mental health advocate, dediated ghostwriter and published author celebrated for the evocative poetry collection, I'm Happy. With a deep-seated passion for writing, literacy, and storytelling, Renee' Blackwell crafts narratives that are whimsical, haunting, sad, dark, and beautiful, resonating deeply with readers. Renee'is a proud supporter of the LGBTQIA+ community, using their platform to champion inclusivity and understanding. @TheReneeBlackwell

Sarahtonin

Sarahtonin, author of Let's Get Naked!, is a 2019 graduate from Sam Houston State University (eat 'em up, Kats!) with a degree in Communication Studies and a minor in Sociology, allowing her to utilize her interests and skill set about human behavior and relationships in her education. Sarahtonin dreams of giving a TED Talk, writing a dystopian novel, and obtaining her Master's in Marriage and Family Counseling. @Sarahtonin621

About the Authors

Skyy Danielle

Skyy Danielle, is a published author and poet. Not only is Skyy a poet. She is the CEO and Founder of Faithful Beauty, LLC; a growing accessory boutique. She is also the author of Faithfully Affirmed and host of Faithfully Affirmed Podcast. An advocate for mental health, healing, women supporting each other and lover of affirmations. Make sure you tap in with her socials as she has so much more in store. @IamSkyyDanielle

Tequila Smith

Tequila Smith has a decade of experience as an esteemed educator. She is the recipient of Katy I.S.D.'s 2023 TEACHER OF THE YEAR! Smith is dedicated to fostering an environment where children are inspired to envision boundless possibilities for their futures. Tequila Smith is the creator of, Igniting Bright Futures, children's books to inspire children silently struggling to accept their differences as beautiful, highly favored, and divinely chosen. @TequilaSmithTheAuthor

www.ingramcontent.com/pod-product-compliance
Lightning Source LLC
Chambersburg PA
CBHW021649120626
46545CB00002B/779